Who Was
Christopher Columbus?

Who Was
Christopher Columbus?

by Bonnie Bader

illustrated by Nancy Harrison

Penguin Workshop

To Lauren and Allie, who have the world
ahead of them to explore—BB

PENGUIN WORKSHOP
An Imprint of Penguin Random House LLC, New York

Text copyright © 2013 by Bonnie Bader. Illustrations copyright © 2013 by Nancy Harrison. Cover illustration copyright © 2013 by Penguin Random House LLC. All rights reserved. Published by Penguin Workshop, an imprint of Penguin Random House LLC, New York. PENGUIN and PENGUIN WORKSHOP are trademarks of Penguin Books Ltd. WHO HQ & Design is a registered trademark of Penguin Random House LLC. Printed in the USA.

Visit us online at www.penguinrandomhouse.com.

Library of Congress Control Number: 2012037715

ISBN 9780448463339   20 19 18 17

Contents

Who Was
Christopher Columbus?

A tall man paced the deck of his ship. He
and his men had been at sea for seventy days,
since August 3, 1492. They had sailed over 2,650
miles from Spain. Now, land had been spotted.
Had Christopher Columbus's dream to reach the
Indies finally come true?

For years he had begged the rulers of Portugal and Spain to give him money for this journey. He wanted to find a route from Europe to the Indies by sailing west. The Indies included China, Japan, and India. No one had done this before.

As the sun rose on October 12, 1492, Columbus and his crew made their way to shore.

Falling to his knees, he kissed the ground and cried. Oh, what riches awaited him! He would return to Spain a hero.

Columbus didn't know that this was not the Indies. So where was he? Columbus and his crew were on land that no one in Europe knew about. Christopher Columbus had discovered a new world.

Chapter 1
An Explorer Is Born

In 1451, a boy named Cristoforo Colombo was born in the city of Genoa, Italy. In the English-speaking world, he is known as Christopher Columbus.

Christopher's father was a wool weaver. His mother was the daughter of a weaver, and she

helped with the work. It was expected that one day Christopher would take over the family business.

But young Christopher did not want to follow in his father's footsteps. He loved the sea, the smell of the salty air. He loved the way the wind blew through his hair. Genoa was a busy port on the Mediterranean Sea. Christopher and his

younger brother, Bartolomeo, loved going down
to the docks. They watched ships come into port,
bringing in goods such as silk, tea, and spices from
the East. And they watched the ships leave, loaded
with wool, copper, tin, and weapons. Christopher
hoped to work on one of those ships one day.

At that time, boys as young as ten went off
to sea as cabin boys. A cabin boy did all sorts
of jobs—cooking, cleaning, fetching tools and
supplies. Christopher got his first job aboard a
ship when he was about fourteen.

Christopher split his time between helping his

father and sailing the seas. He sailed to such places as Ireland and Iceland. He learned a lot about how to steer a ship in the open sea. This skill would be very important later in his life.

At nineteen, Christopher had grown into a strong young man. No one knows exactly what he looked like. Some say he was tall with wide shoulders. His skin was said to be pale, and he is believed to have had red hair and light blue eyes. Not only was his body strong, but his mind was sharp. Some said he was too stubborn and had a bad temper. He was also very, very sure of himself. Once he set his mind on something, he never let it go. And Christopher Columbus was very sure about one thing—he wanted to become a famous sea captain. Famous and rich.

Chapter 2
Mapping the World

In 1476, when Christopher was twenty-five years old, he was on a ship attacked by French warships. The ship went up in flames. But Christopher managed to reach the shore.

He was near a small fishing village in Portugal. Some villagers found him and took care of him. Christopher was happy for their help. However, he did not want to stay in a quiet village. He soon made his way to the capital city of Lisbon.

For nine years he lived in Lisbon. His brother Bartolomeo lived there, too, and they opened a business together. They were mapmakers. This was a perfect job for a man who wanted to learn more about the world. At the docks, the brothers would meet the captains of incoming ships. They would collect information and create maps based on what the captains told them.

At the map store, Christopher heard merchants talking about trying to find a new route from Europe to eastern lands known as the Indies. Why were these merchants so interested in traveling there? Spices. Spices such as pepper, ginger, cloves, and cinnamon. People used spices in cooking to flavor food. In Egypt, Italian merchants could buy spices from the Indies. Then they sold them all over Europe for a lot of money. But if an explorer found a route directly to the Indies, he could buy up spices. There would be no need to rely on the

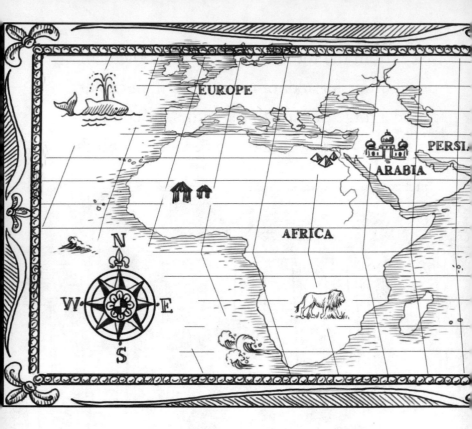

Italian merchants. Whoever found a sea route to the Indies would grow rich from the spice trade.

At that time, most people knew the world was round. What they didn't know was how big it was. It was thought that one landmass—Europe and Asia and Africa—was surrounded by one body of water called the Ocean Sea.

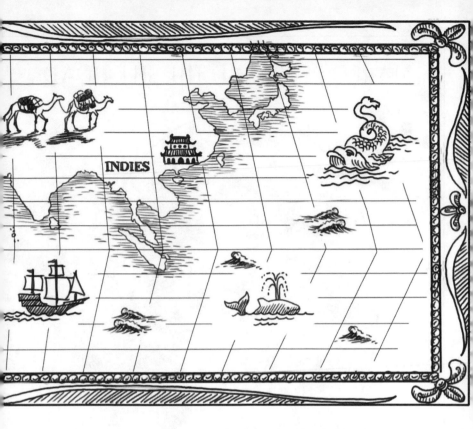

The only travelers so far to reach the Indies had gone by land. *The Description of the World*, written by the explorer Marco Polo, told of his travels from Italy to China. Columbus read the book. He was fascinated by Marco Polo's stories of rubies as big as a man's fist, and palaces with floors made of gold.

MARCO POLO AND THE SILK ROAD

IN 1260, TWO BROTHERS, MARCO AND NICCOLÒ POLO, TRAVELED EAST, OVERLAND, FROM EUROPE TO CHINA. (IN THOSE DAYS, CHINA WAS PART OF THE MONGOL EMPIRE.) IN 1265, THEY ARRIVED IN CHINA AND MET THE RULER, KUBLAI KHAN. OVER THE NEXT TWO HUNDRED YEARS, TRADE BETWEEN

INDIA, CHINA, AND EUROPE GREW. MERCHANTS
TRAVELED THE OVERLAND ROUTE, KNOWN AS
THE SILK ROAD, AND TRADED GOODS SUCH AS
SILK, PEARLS, GOLD, RUBIES, PEPPER, NUTMEG,
CLOVES, AND TEA. BUT THE ROAD WAS LONG AND
DANGEROUS. TRAVELERS HAD TO CROSS DESERTS
AND MOUNTAINS. BANDITS WAITED TO ROB THEM
OF THEIR GOODS. BY THE FIFTEENTH CENTURY,
EUROPEANS DESPERATELY WANTED TO FIND
ANOTHER WAY TO THE INDIES.

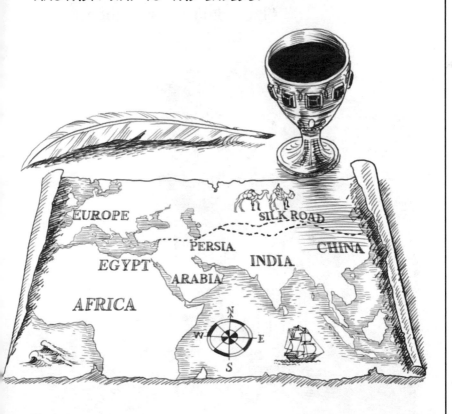

Columbus was determined to be the first to *sail* all the way to the Indies. The king of Portugal had tried to send ships to the Indies by following a route around Africa, then east. But the ships kept turning back. The sailors said this route was too long. And they did not know where they were going. But Columbus had another idea. A *better* idea, he thought. He would sail *west* to the Indies. He would sail straight across the Ocean Sea!

Other people laughed at his plan. Sail across the Ocean Sea? Why, that would take months! Columbus wouldn't be able to take along enough food and water. How would he and the crew survive?

Christopher had no answer for these questions. So he read more. He read book after book about traveling the world. One book said there were only three thousand nautical miles between the Canary Islands and Japan. Japan was a place in the Indies where Columbus wanted to go!

Another book about the Indies claimed there were men with umbrella-shaped feet, people with eyes on their shoulders, and creatures that were

half lion and half eagle! Most people thought these stories were made up. Still, the more Columbus read, the more excited he became.

Even more important to Christopher Columbus was his belief that God meant for him to make the journey to the Indies. He believed God had given him the love of the sea. God had brought him to Portugal. And God would guide him in his travels.

Chapter 3
Waiting and More Waiting

What Christopher needed was someone to give him the money for his trip. Someone who was rich. And powerful. Someone like the king of Portugal. But how would Christopher meet the king? He needed an in, a connection.

In 1478, Christopher Columbus

KING JOHN II OF PORTUGAL

married Felipa Perestrello e Moniz. Her family had friends at the king's court.

But it wasn't until 1484 that Christopher Columbus finally met King John II of Portugal. Columbus stood tall in front of the king. He told him he knew the right way to get to the Indies. He was sure of it. And Columbus promised to bring back lots and lots of gold. King John listened to this big talker. And what did the king say? He said no.

Christopher Columbus was not discouraged. If the king of Portugal wouldn't support him, maybe King Ferdinand and Queen Isabella of Spain would.

While Christopher was waiting to meet King John, his wife had died. So when Christopher went to Spain, he left their young son, Diego, in the  care of monks at a monastery. A young boy would not survive a dangerous journey across the sea.

Columbus had to wait nine months to see Queen Isabella and King Ferdinand. Why? In those days, the Spanish royal court moved from city to city. Columbus could not afford to follow the court, so he settled in the city of Córdoba to wait. There he met a young peasant girl named Beatriz Enríquez de Harana. Two years later, Beatriz gave birth to Columbus's second son, a boy named Ferdinand.

Then, finally, on May 1, 1486, Columbus got to meet King Ferdinand and Queen Isabella. He was hopeful that the king and queen would say yes to the voyage. They would see what a good

Christian Columbus was. He would spread the faith throughout the new lands. Plus, his trip would help make Spain very rich.

But Spain was in the middle of a costly war. There was no money now for a long trip to the Indies. Columbus would have to wait. More waiting? Oh no!

Two years went by. Columbus tried asking King John II of Portugal for money again. But he was too busy—busy celebrating the return of another explorer, Bartholomew Diaz. Columbus's plan to sail west still seemed foolish to King John.

So it was back to Spain for Columbus. The war Ferdinand and Isabella were fighting went on for three more years. All that time, Columbus waited. And when he went back to see the king and queen, at last he got the answer he was waiting for.

Yes!

Columbus was now forty-one years old. That was old to be setting out on such a hard journey.

BARTHOLOMEW DIAZ

ANXIOUS TO FIND A TRADE ROUTE TO INDIA, KING JOHN II OF PORTUGAL SENT BARTHOLOMEW DIAZ ON A VOYAGE. DIAZ LEFT LISBON IN AUGUST 1487. DESPITE TERRIBLE WEATHER, HE AND HIS CREW

BARTHOLOMEW DIAZ

REALIZED THAT IT WAS POSSIBLE TO SAIL AROUND THE SOUTHERN TIP OF AFRICA. THEY CALLED IT THE CAPE OF STORMS, BECAUSE OF THE TERRIBLE WEATHER THEY ENCOUNTERED THERE. (IT WAS LATER RENAMED THE CAPE OF GOOD HOPE.) DIAZ RETURNED TO PORTUGAL IN 1488, A HERO. ALTHOUGH HE DIDN'T SAIL ALL THE WAY AROUND THE TIP OF AFRICA—VASCO DA GAMA DID THAT IN 1497—DIAZ WAS CREDITED WITH HELPING TO OPEN UP A NEW TRADE ROUTE WITH THE EAST.

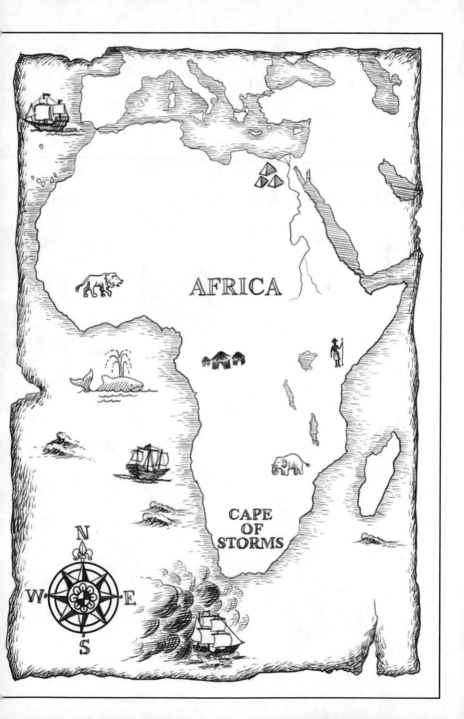

He was angry about the long years of waiting. So he made some demands.

What did he want? Well, if he was successful, he wanted the title of Admiral of the Ocean Sea. He wanted to rule all the lands he discovered. And he wanted to be able to keep one-tenth of any treasure he found there.

Queen Isabella did not believe what she was hearing. Who was this arrogant man? She would not give in to his demands. No, Queen Isabella was through with Christopher Columbus!

So what did Christopher Columbus do? He packed his bags, saddled up his mule, and went to see the king of France. Maybe he would send Columbus on the voyage.

As Columbus started on his way, he heard hoofbeats behind him. It was Queen Isabella's men. She had changed her mind. She wasn't about to let the king of France get riches that could be hers. And if Columbus failed, well, then nothing would be lost; neither Isabella nor the French king would get a thing. A contract was signed.

Columbus's journey was about to begin.

Chapter 4
On the Ocean Sea

Now Christopher Columbus needed ships and a crew. Queen Isabella ordered the people from the town of Palos to give Columbus two ships. Palos had supported her enemies in the war, and she wanted to punish the town.

It was expensive to make ships. But the townspeople had to obey her.

The two ships from Palos were called the *Niña* and the *Pinta*. They were caravels—small but fast. But Columbus also wanted something bigger. He looked and looked. The biggest ship he could find, the sixty-foot-long *Santa María*, was a slow cargo boat. Still he decided to make do.

THE NAO AND THE CARAVEL

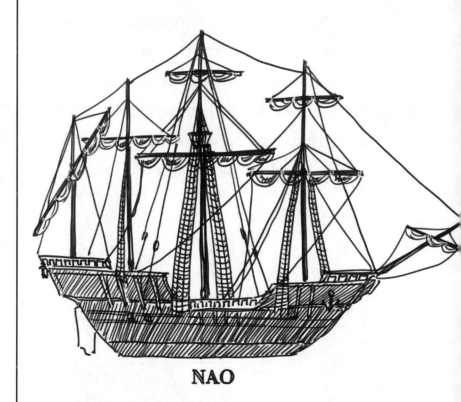

NAO

THE NAO (PRONOUNCE IT LIKE THIS: *NOW*) AND
THE CARAVEL WERE TWO TYPES OF SHIPS THAT
COULD SAIL LONG DISTANCES. THE NAO WAS A BIG,
HEAVY, SLOW SHIP WITH THREE OR FOUR MASTS.
IT WAS GOOD FOR CARRYING CARGO. IT WAS ALSO
STABLE ON ROUGH SEAS. AND IT HAD A LOT OF

ROOM, SO A LOT OF FOOD AND WATER COULD BE
STORED FOR LONG VOYAGES. THE CARAVEL WAS
A NEWER TYPE OF SHIP. IT HAD ONE TO THREE
MASTS AND WAS LIGHTER THAN THE NAO.

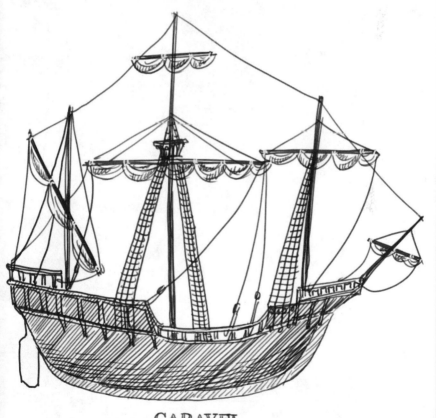

CARAVEL

Two brothers from Palos, Martín and Vicente Pinzón, signed on to serve as captains. Martín would command the *Pinta*, Vicente the *Niña*. Columbus would be the captain of the *Santa María*. He was also in charge of the entire fleet.

As for the crew, it was hard to find men willing to go. Most people thought Columbus's idea to sail west was crazy.

After begging, pleading, and even threatening, Columbus got about ninety men to join his crew. Many were friends or relatives of the Pinzón brothers. Others were criminals. They were freed from jail to sail with Columbus. Twenty-four men were to sail on the *Niña*, twenty-six on the *Pinta*, and forty on the *Santa María*.

Most of the men were sailors. But there were also men to repair the ships, men to fish, men to clean, and men to make barrels. Columbus also took along a secretary and a doctor. No women were on board. (In those days, no women were sailors.)

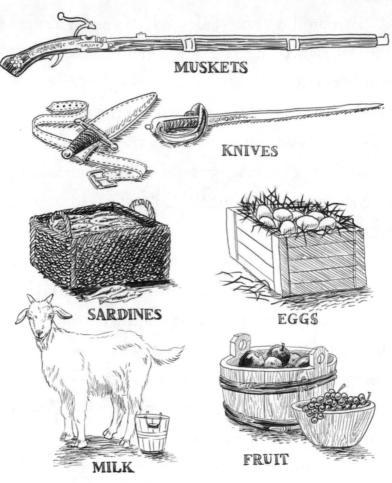

MUSKETS

KNIVES

SARDINES

EGGS

MILK

FRUIT

The ships were loaded with supplies. Ropes and maps and compasses. Fresh and dried meat, milk, fruit, eggs, sardines, anchovies, olive oil, raisins, biscuits, cheese, peas, garlic, onions, rice,

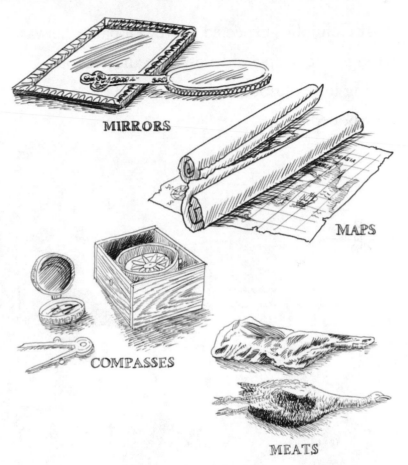

MIRRORS

MAPS

COMPASSES

MEATS

and beans. And many barrels of water. They took cannons, crossbows, and muskets in case of run-ins with enemy ships. And for trading, they took bells, scissors, knives, coins, beads, and mirrors.

If Columbus expected a farewell party, he was wrong. The people of Palos were angry about paying for Columbus's ships. Instead of cheering, they booed.

It was August 2, 1492. Christopher Columbus gathered his men onshore to pray. They prayed for a safe journey. They prayed that they would find new lands and riches.

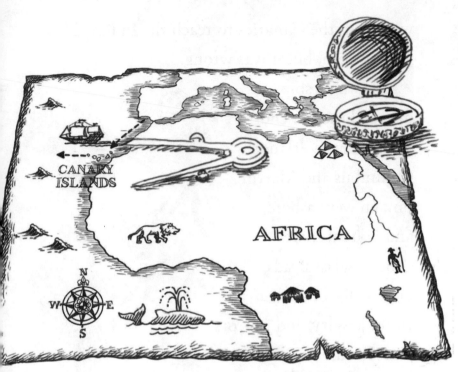

Then, in the early hours of August 3, 1492, the *Niña*, the *Pinta*, and the *Santa María* set sail from Palos. Columbus's plan was to sail south to the Canary Islands. From there, he would turn west, toward Cipangu (known today as Japan). Columbus thought that the path from the Canary Islands to Cipangu would follow a straight line. He thought that he just had to sail 2,400 miles west from the Canaries to reach the Indies. That was his plan, but it was wrong.

The three ships dropped their anchors at the Canary Islands. Columbus and Martín Pinzón went ashore and bought more goods—glass beads, brass bells, brightly dyed cloth, jewelry, and mirrors. These could be traded in the Indies. They also loaded the ships with fresh food.

On September 6, 1492, they set sail once again. Columbus led the way in the *Santa María*. The first few days on the open sea were smooth sailing. The men seemed happy. They sang songs and fished off the sides of the ships. And when the sun set, the men gathered together and prayed.

The crew slept in two shifts. One crew worked during the day. The other crew worked at night.

But as the days went by, the crew grew restless. They had been at sea a long time. Just how far had they come? Well, Columbus kept two logbooks. In one, he recorded the real distance sailed each day. In the other— the one that his crew could look at—he recorded fewer miles. According to Columbus, he didn't want to scare the crew by letting them think the voyage was taking too long.

But the men were scared, anyway. They were out in the middle of the ocean. What would they find? Would they ever return home? So Columbus kept talking about all the riches that awaited them.

The men were on the lookout for any sign of land. Anything gave them hope. A bit of seaweed on the water. Birds flying together.

On September 25, Martín Pinzón thought he saw land. But no, he hadn't.

For more than two weeks more, the ships sailed on. Most of the men had never been on a trip that lasted so long. To them, those weeks seemed like forever!

And life on the ship was not pleasant. Columbus's crew did not bathe or brush their teeth. They walked the deck in their bare feet. Sometimes, they stepped on a bug or a rat dropping. And what happened when they needed to go to the bathroom? They went over the side of the ship!

On each ship, the only cabin was for the captain. The rest of the crew slept wherever they could find a dry spot—on top of a coil of rope or next to a barrel.

There were no cooks. The men had to prepare
food themselves. But first they had to battle
the mice and rats that tried to get the food!
Sometimes, fish were caught and salted and dried.
If the crew wanted to make biscuits, they would
first have to pick insects out of the flour. Most
of the time, the food was rotten or didn't taste
good. So they put a lot of garlic in it to hide the
bad taste. And they usually ate at night so they
wouldn't have to see what was crawling around in
their food!

The ships were very dirty. Rats scurried over
the wooden planks. Fleas were everywhere.
And there were lice. Everyone got lice!

The mood aboard the ships got worse each day. Some of the men thought Columbus was going crazy. They had seen him pacing the deck, staring at the sky. Where was this madman taking them? Some men wanted to toss Columbus overboard. Then they could head home.

On October 7, there was another false sighting of land. Columbus now promised that if land wasn't reached in three days, he would turn the fleet around.

Luckily, on the night of October 10, Columbus thought he saw land.

This time it was true. Just after midnight on October 12, a crewmember from the *Pinta* shouted, *"Tierra! Tierra!"* (Land! Land!)

Yes, the faint outline of land could be seen. Everyone rejoiced. They had reached the Indies. Or so they thought.

Chapter 5
Land Ho!

As soon as the sun rose on October 12, Columbus was ready to go ashore. He and his officers put on their best clothes and piled into small rowboats. They had a Spanish flag and items to trade. They also took swords and knives, in case they met unfriendly natives.

What riches were they about to find? Gold? Spices?

Columbus stepped onto the strange land, fell to his knees, and kissed the ground. He thanked God for leading him here. Columbus planted the flag and claimed the land for Spain. He named it San Salvador.

Watching Columbus from behind bushes were some of the island's native inhabitants. They were called the Taino. Slowly, they crept closer. Columbus and his men stared at these strange people. They were not wearing gold and silk. In fact, they were hardly wearing anything at all!

The natives were equally surprised. The Taino had never seen white men or people wearing clothes or people with beards. And the ships out in the sea? How strange they were!

THE TAINO

THE TAINO PEOPLE WERE RULED BY A CHIEF.
IT COULD BE A MAN OR A WOMAN. FAMILIES LIVED
IN BUILDINGS MADE FROM WOODEN POLES, WOVEN
STRAW, AND LEAVES. THE TAINO WERE EXCELLENT
FARMERS, FISHERMEN, AND HUNTERS. THEY WERE
ALSO SKILLED WOOD-CARVERS, AND THEY WOVE
BEAUTIFUL HAMMOCKS OUT OF COTTON. THEY
WORSHIPPED MANY DIFFERENT GODS. COLUMBUS
BELIEVED HIS MISSION WAS TO CONVERT THEM
ALL TO CHRISTIANITY. THE TAINO LIVED HAPPILY
AND PEACEFULLY BEFORE COLUMBUS ARRIVED.
EUROPEANS BROUGHT DISEASES SUCH AS
SMALLPOX, MEASLES, AND THE FLU. IN THIRTY
YEARS, BETWEEN 80 AND 90 PERCENT OF THE
TAINO DIED.

Columbus thought this island was off the coast of the Indies. So he called the people he met "Indians." Of course, the island was nowhere near the Indies. Columbus's ships had actually landed in what is today known as the Bahamas. The island of San Salvador was beautiful. Lush trees, winding rivers, a big sparkling lake.

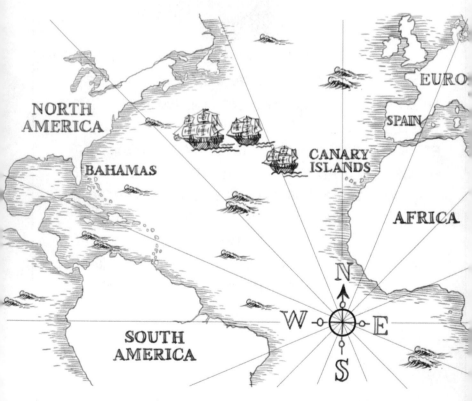

The Taino gave the Spaniards cotton, wooden spears, and parrots. Lots and lots of colorful and noisy parrots! In return, the Taino got glass beads and bells.

But where were the palaces with gold floors? Where were all the riches and spices? Columbus saw that some Taino had small gold rings in their noses. There must be gold somewhere, Columbus reasoned.

WHY GOLD?

GOLD HAS ALWAYS BEEN VALUABLE BECAUSE IT IS SO RARE AND BEAUTIFUL. BETWEEN THE YEARS 1370 AND 1420, MANY BIG GOLD MINES IN EUROPE RAN OUT OF GOLD. SO EUROPEAN MERCHANTS BEGAN TRAVELING TO AFRICA AND ASIA IN SEARCH OF GOLD. THE RACE TO FIND GOLD WAS FIERCE. LATER, IN 1511 (AFTER COLUMBUS'S DEATH), KING FERDINAND PROCLAIMED, "GET GOLD, HUMANELY IF YOU CAN, BUT AT ALL HAZARDS, GET GOLD!" IN A SHORT TIME, THE INCA AND AZTEC CIVILIZATIONS IN CENTRAL AMERICA, WHICH WERE RICH WITH GOLD, WERE DESTROYED BY SPANISH CONQUERORS.

Columbus tried using signs and gestures to communicate. He waved his arms and asked where the gold was. Through signs, the natives told him there was an island to the south that had gold. That must be China, Columbus thought.

On October 14, Columbus and his crew set off. But before they pulled up their anchors, they kidnapped several Taino and took them on board. These men would be taught Spanish and could serve as interpreters on the other islands.

The *Niña*, *Pinta*, and *Santa María* spent two weeks sailing around different islands. They met many friendly natives. They were given a lot of cotton and spears and parrots. But no gold.

Columbus turned to the Indians for help. They signed for him to sail south to another island. Columbus thought they were talking about Japan. On October 28, the *Niña*, the *Pinta,* and the *Santa María* arrived at this next island. When Columbus saw natives wearing gold around their wrists and ankles, he became excited. This wasn't Japan, Columbus decided. It was China! Even better!

Once again, Columbus was wrong. He was actually in Cuba. Columbus sent a group of men to introduce themselves to the famous ruler of China, the Great Khan. But of course the group came back with no sign of the Great Khan. Worse yet, there was no gold here. It was time to move on.

Chapter 6
Shipwreck!

By early December, the *Pinta* had gone off on its own to find gold. The weather was turning colder and stormy. If the *Niña* and the *Santa María* were to return to Spain before winter set in, they had to leave soon.

But there was still more to explore, Columbus thought, so he ordered his ships to sail. On December 6, Columbus named the island they landed on Hispaniola, because the trees there reminded him of Spain.

Then on Christmas Eve, disaster struck. Some men were celebrating. After a long night, Columbus went to sleep. So did most of the crew of the *Santa María*. One of the ship's boys was left in charge.

The wind was calm. And the ship was moving at a slow pace. Yet, sometime after midnight, the *Santa María* crashed into a coral reef. A cry rang out and Columbus was awoken. Desperately, he tried to save the ship. But it was too late. Her sides had ripped open.

The *Santa María* was sinking!

Columbus called for help. A local Taino chief sent men in canoes. They unloaded the *Santa María*, and brought the goods and supplies ashore.

Besides helping unload the ship, the natives brought gold! Not a lot, just a few samples— masks, jewelry, and other small trinkets.

After he got over the shock of losing a ship, Columbus took the sinking of the *Santa María* as a sign. God meant for him to go ashore on this island. After all, the chief had given Columbus rings, necklaces, and masks made of gold. And gold was what he had come for! Perhaps now they could go home.

But Columbus only had one ship left. Martín Pinzón and the *Pinta* were still missing. They couldn't all return to Spain on the small *Niña*. So Columbus built a fort. Forty men would remain there through the winter. They would look for gold. When Columbus returned, he would bring them (and the gold) home.

Columbus used wood from the *Santa María* to build the fort. A moat was dug around the fort, and the *Santa María*'s cannons were put up. Columbus named the fort La Navidad. That is Spanish for "Christmas."

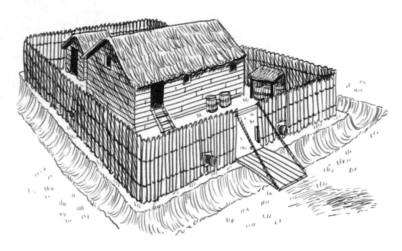

The *Niña* was loaded with fresh food and water. With what little gold he had, Columbus headed home on January 4, 1493.

After two days at sea, the *Niña* came upon an amazing sight. The *Pinta*! The two ships met and continued the voyage home together until a bad storm separated them again.

Columbus feared that the *Pinta* might be lost forever. The storm grew fiercer. What if they drowned? Then nobody would know that the voyage had been successful. So Columbus grabbed a piece of parchment and wrote about his discovery of new lands. He wrapped the letter in cloth, covered it in a cake of wax, and placed

it in a barrel.
Hopefully, one
day, someone
would find the
barrel and read

about what Columbus had accomplished.

The storm raged for fifteen days. Even so,
Columbus sailed on. After all, what choice did he
have?

On March 15, Columbus dropped anchor in
the waters of Palos. It had been almost seven and
a half months since he had last seen this beautiful
harbor. What joy he must have felt. And,
amazingly, the *Pinta* had also made it home safely.

Of course, King Ferdinand and Queen Isabella
wanted to see Columbus right away. So he set off
for Barcelona. Everywhere, people ran out into
the streets to catch a glimpse of Columbus and
his crew. The people had never seen Indians or
parrots or corn before.

At last, Columbus reached the royal court. There, under a golden canopy, sat Ferdinand and Isabella. As Columbus approached the king and queen, the royal couple stood up! Only a great lord would receive such a greeting. Columbus kissed their hands and sat down next to them. Then he described his journey. Columbus showed off the treasures he had brought back. Colorful parrots. Gold nose rings. Not a lot of gold, to be sure. But some. And he had brought corn. Yams. Yucca. No one was laughing at Christopher Columbus now.

Best of all, the king and queen kept their word.
Columbus was given the title Admiral of the
Ocean Sea. He was made governor-general of all
the lands he discovered. And he got to keep one-
tenth of all the treasure he had brought back.

Christopher Columbus was a hero. He rode through Barcelona seated next to the king. People cheered. This was the greatest moment of his life. Soon, his glory days would be over.

Chapter 7
On the Sea Again

Orders were given for Columbus's second trip. He was to return to Hispaniola, bring back the crew left there, and leave more men to settle the land.

Columbus was elated. Here was another chance to bring back gold.

On his first voyage, Columbus practically had to beg men to join him. This time, between 1,200 and 1,500 men eagerly volunteered. Who knew what riches would be found on the trip?

Now the crew included priests (to convert the natives),

noblemen, farmers, and other skilled laborers. Even Columbus's younger brother Diego signed on.

Columbus was given seventeen ships. The *Niña* was part of the fleet. Columbus commanded a ship called the *Santa María* in honor of the one that had been wrecked.

The ships were loaded with food and water. This time horses were brought along for the men to use once they reached land, as well as sheep

and pigs to live on farms, and seeds of wheat and barley to plant.

On September 25, 1493, the ships set off from

the port of Cadiz. This time, it was a much easier
trip across the ocean. Columbus knew the way.
No one complained.

THE ISLANDS OF COLUMBUS'S SECOND VOYAGE

ON HIS WAY BACK TO HISPANIOLA, COLUMBUS AND HIS CREW STOPPED AT MANY ISLANDS. YOU CAN SEE SOME OF THEM ON THIS MAP. DOMINICA WAS THE FIRST ISLAND THEY CAME TO. COLUMBUS NAMED IT DOMINICA BECAUSE IT WAS DISCOVERED ON A SUNDAY (NOVEMBER 3, 1493). ON GUADELOUPE, COLUMBUS AND HIS MEN TASTED PINEAPPLE FOR THE FIRST TIME. SANTA MARIA LA REDONDA WAS THE "ROUND ISLAND." HE ALSO DISCOVERED THE VIRGIN ISLANDS AND PUERTO RICO.

Columbus checked out new islands. He found cotton, more colorful parrots, and fruit. And, oh, the scenery! Green mountains. Wide valleys. Sparkling rivers. Foamy white waterfalls. But they also saw awful things. Women were captured and made slaves. Humans ate other humans. (They are called cannibals.) Columbus and his crew didn't stay very long on those islands!

On the night of November 27, 1493, the ships arrived in Hispaniola. Right away, one of the ships fired a cannon. There was no response from the shore. Where were the men who had stayed behind? What could have happened to them? Columbus and his crew were scared.

Suddenly, they heard the sound of oars slapping the water. Could it be Columbus's men? No. It was a canoe filled with Taino. And they were bringing terrible news. The fort had burned down. All the Spaniards were dead. What had happened? It was unclear. Some said the

Spaniards fought among themselves and killed
each other. Others said the settlers had gotten sick
and died. Still others claimed a nearby tribe killed
the Spaniards and burned down the settlement.
Whatever the true story was, La Navidad was gone.
A new settlement had to be built from scratch.

In a hot, swampy area with no clean water,
Columbus and his crew began to build a new
colony. They called it Isabella in honor of their

queen. It was a bad spot to choose. Mosquitoes and gnats swarmed around the men, biting their flesh.

The men were not happy. This was not why they had come on the voyage. They wanted gold. To make matters worse, many men fell ill. Perhaps they got sick from the bug bites. Perhaps it was because there wasn't enough food to eat.

The crops they planted weren't growing well. Or maybe they were just plain tired.

There was no choice but to send some of the fleet back to Spain for food and medicine. So on February 2, 1494, twelve ships returned home.

Columbus remained behind. Why? His desire to find gold made him stay. He sent many groups of healthy men to search for it. But each time, they came back empty-handed. They found specks of gold here and there in riverbeds. But not nearly enough to satisfy the king and queen.

Word reached Columbus of rich goldfields at a place called Cibao. So Columbus left his brother Diego in charge of Isabella and set off. Some gold was found, but just as before, not a lot.

Where was Cipangu, the island that Marco Polo had described? For the first time, Columbus was starting to grow nervous.

Columbus took three ships and sailed back to Cuba as well as to other islands he had visited.

When Columbus returned to Hispaniola at the end of September 1494, he was very ill. And he still didn't have much gold.

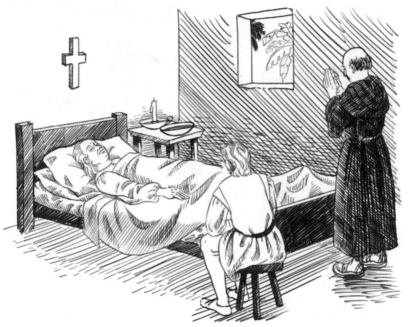

Back at Isabella, the mosquitoes seemed to have gotten larger. His men were getting sicker. And angrier. Things were worse for the Taino, too. Columbus demanded that the Taino find gold for him. Every adult had to supply a certain amount of it or face severe punishment.

The Taino tried to fight back.
However, their simple
swords, bows,
and arrows were
no match for
the Spaniards'
weapons. They
had crossbows
and muskets.

With no gold for King Ferdinand and Queen
Isabella, Columbus decided to take many Taino
back to Spain as slaves. It was a terrible thing to
do. But Columbus felt that it was his right. After
all, he had claimed the land for Spain. So wasn't
it his right to claim the people, too? The answer,
of course, was no—it wasn't his right. Still,
Columbus loaded ships with five hundred Taino
and sent them off to Spain. Perhaps the slaves
could be sold at market and bring in money.

Columbus was also nervous because he knew

that word had gotten back to Ferdinand and
Isabella that Columbus was not a good leader. He
was stubborn. And arrogant.

Columbus concluded that he had to return to
Spain to defend himself. Nothing that was going
wrong was his fault. Perhaps God was
punishing him.

Columbus put his brothers Bartolomeo and Diego in charge of Isabella. It was March 10, 1496. He loaded up two small ships. Raising the anchors, Columbus headed back to Spain.

Chapter 8
A Third Try

The return trip was rough. There were strong winds and high seas. The trip took four months, longer than expected. Supplies ran short. When Columbus reached Cadiz in July 1496, he and his

men looked as though they had been through a war. They were hungry and tired. Their clothes hung on their bodies like rags.

Columbus defended himself before King

Ferdinand and Queen Isabella. He told them
he had brought back some treasure. (This was
true.) And he said he had explored seven hundred
islands. (This was an exaggeration!)

The king and queen were not happy. Columbus had failed. He had not brought back what he had promised. Members of the court called him "Admiral of the Mosquitoes." Columbus's sons, Diego and Ferdinand, were there. They served as pages to the king and queen. They had to watch as their father was disgraced.

Yet, two years later, the king and queen agreed to send Columbus on another voyage. Why did they do this?

An explorer from Portugal, Vasco da Gama, had actually reached the Indies. He had sailed down the west coast of Africa, around the tip of the continent, and on to India. He brought back many riches. The rulers of Spain did not want Portugal getting all the treasure. So they decided to take another chance. Maybe Columbus, on this next voyage sailing west, would strike it rich . . . finally.

Forty-six-year-old Columbus began his fourth

CHRISTOPHER COLUMBUS

voyage from southern Spain on May 30, 1498. He had just six ships. Sure, it was a larger fleet than his first voyage. But once again, his crew was made up of many criminals. Why? Because people had heard of Columbus's failures. No one wanted to sail with him!

The ships sailed southwest to the Canary Islands. There they split into two groups. Three ships went to Hispaniola to deliver supplies. The other three, under Columbus's command, went off exploring. Once again Columbus ran into trouble. There was no wind, so they just floated. The sun was hot, so the men's skin blistered. Their food began to rot, and their water barrels burst in the

blazing heat. The heat
lasted for eight days.

Then the winds picked up, and land was
spotted. Columbus must have been overjoyed. He
named this island Trinidad after the Holy Trinity.

Just across from this island lay what could
have been Columbus's biggest discovery—the

coastline of South America. The land looked like a continent. But how could that be? Columbus was still sure that he had already found the Indies. Columbus reasoned that what he saw now must be the "Earthly Paradise," or the Garden of Eden. He had no time to explore this paradise though; he wanted to get back to Hispaniola.

VASCO DA GAMA

WHEN VASCO DA GAMA DECIDED TO TRY REACHING THE INDIES BY SAILING AROUND AFRICA, MANY PEOPLE THOUGHT HE WAS CRAZY. THEY DID NOT THINK THAT THE ATLANTIC OCEAN CONNECTED WITH THE INDIAN OCEAN. (BARTHOLOMEW DIAZ HAD SAILED TO THE TIP OF AFRICA, BUT NOT AROUND IT.) ON JULY 8, 1497, DA GAMA SET SAIL FROM LISBON AND PROVED THAT THE OCEANS DID INDEED CONNECT. HE GUIDED HIS SHIPS AROUND AFRICA'S

VASCO DE GAMA

CAPE OF GOOD HOPE ON NOVEMBER 22, 1497.
AFTER MAKING STOPS IN AFRICA, VASCO DA GAMA
REACHED CALICUT, INDIA, ON MAY 20, 1498. HE
TRADED GOODS WITH THE PEOPLE OF INDIA. ON
THE RETURN TRIP, MANY OF HIS CREWMEMBERS
DIED FROM SCURVY, A DISEASE CAUSED BY A LACK
OF VITAMIN C. NONETHELESS, UPON ARRIVING
IN PORTUGAL, VASCO DA GAMA WAS GREETED
AS A HERO.

Arriving in Santo Domingo (a new colony his brothers had established), Columbus was greeted by another nasty surprise. Bartolomeo and Diego were no longer in command. There was no food. People were sick. Some had rebelled. Columbus tried to maintain order. He had no better luck than his brothers.

That August, the king and queen sent someone to see exactly what was going on. He reported back. The rumors were true. Things were a mess. Many men were sick. Others—ones who had rebelled—were dead or in jail. Columbus and his brothers were arrested. Shackles were slapped around their wrists and ankles. They were thrown in jail.

Christopher Columbus, Admiral of the Ocean Sea, was sent back to Spain in chains.

AMERIGO VESPUCCI

AMERIGO VESPUCCI

AMERIGO VESPUCCI IS THE EXPLORER AFTER WHOM NORTH AND SOUTH AMERICA ARE NAMED. HE WAS BORN IN FLORENCE, ITALY, IN 1454 AND MOVED TO SEVILLE, SPAIN. HEARING ABOUT COLUMBUS'S VOYAGES MADE VESPUCCI EAGER TO FIND A WESTERN PASSAGE TO THE INDIES. HE LEARNED TO SAIL AND NAVIGATE, MAKING SEVERAL TRIPS TO PLACES SUCH AS VENEZUELA AND BRAZIL. HE RIGHTLY CONCLUDED THAT THIS

WAS NOT ASIA, DESPITE WHAT COLUMBUS HAD
THOUGHT. VESPUCCI REALIZED THAT THESE PLACES
WERE PART OF A NEW CONTINENT. HE HAD NEW
MAPS DRAWN UP. A GERMAN MAPMAKER SUGGESTED
THAT THIS NEW WORLD BE CALLED AMERICA.

Chapter 9
One Last Try

In Spain, Columbus landed in jail. There he stayed for six weeks. When his chains were taken off, he kept them. He told one of his sons that he wanted to be buried with them.

Most men wouldn't have had the nerve to ask the king and queen for more money for yet another voyage. But Christopher Columbus was not most men. He refused to give up.

The king and queen knew that Vasco da Gama was off on another voyage. He might come back with all sorts of treasure. Why should Portugal get all the glory? So, when Columbus went to Ferdinand and Isabella asking to be sent on a fourth voyage, believe it or not, they said yes. This time, though, they only provided four old ships and 135 men, including Columbus's thirteen year-old son, Ferdinand. And there were rules: No slaves. No stopping off at Hispaniola.

Columbus didn't mind about the rules: All he cared about was going to sea again.

On May 9, 1502, Columbus and his four rickety ships set off. At first, everything was perfect. The sky was clear. The sun was shining.

The stars twinkled at night. And a steady wind moved the ships along. But then the clouds rolled in. The wind picked up. Columbus sniffed the heavy air.

A hurricane was on its way!

The only sensible thing to do was to seek shelter on the nearest island. That was Hispaniola. But Columbus had been forbidden to set foot there. The new governor refused to let him come ashore. Columbus was outraged. This was the place he had settled! Yet he and his men were forced to stay on their ships and wait out the storm.

Columbus next set sail for Jamaica, only to be hit by more storms. One lasted for eighty-eight days. At last, Columbus's ships limped to land—what is modern-day Nicaragua—where they stopped for repairs.

Then, finally, north of what is now Panama, Columbus found gold. At long last! He started another settlement. At first, the natives were friendly. They traded, and the two groups lived alongside each other in peace. But not for long.

In the spring, four hundred natives appeared carrying bows and arrows. A battle began that lasted for three hours. In the end, seven Spaniards and ten natives lay dead.

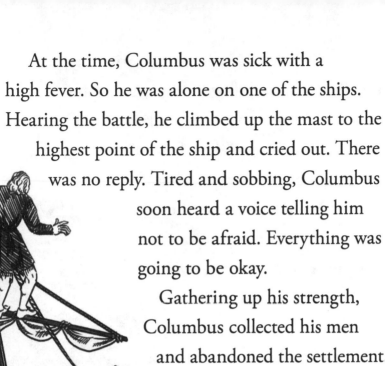

At the time, Columbus was sick with a
high fever. So he was alone on one of the ships.
Hearing the battle, he climbed up the mast to the
highest point of the ship and cried out. There
was no reply. Tired and sobbing, Columbus
soon heard a voice telling him
not to be afraid. Everything was
going to be okay.

Gathering up his strength,
Columbus collected his men
and abandoned the settlement.
He left with a couple ships
that were in such terrible
shape, they were
practically in pieces.
They anchored off the coast
of Jamaica. And that
was where they stayed
for the next year.

Columbus and his

men were stranded. At least the natives seemed friendly. Each day, they brought Columbus and his men food to eat and water to drink. But Columbus did not trust them. What if the natives stopped bringing food? Or worse, what if they attacked? This time, there were no ships to escape on.

Columbus convinced two of his men, Diego Méndez and Bartolomeo Fieschi, to take a canoe and paddle to Hispaniola. There they could buy a ship and come back to rescue them. At first Méndez thought this was an impossible plan. But he took the risk, anyway. Columbus kissed Méndez on both his cheeks and bid him and Fieschi a safe journey.

A few days after Méndez and Fieschi left, Columbus's fears about the natives proved true. They refused to bring any more supplies. So

Columbus decided to trick the natives into doing what he wanted. Knowing that there would soon be a lunar eclipse, Columbus told them God was very angry with them. It was wrong to stop bringing food and water. God was so angry, in fact, that he was going to hide the moon. When the eclipse appeared that night, and the moon did indeed "hide," the natives were scared. They promised to keep bringing food. And they did until the day the rescue ship arrived.

On June 29, 1504, a very old ship sailed to the coast of Jamaica. Christopher Columbus was almost fifty-two years old. Now his eyesight was

failing. He was in poor health and in constant pain. Still, he was happy to be rescued. And he was anxious to get home to see the queen.

But he never set eyes on Queen Isabella again. Three weeks after his arrival in Spain, the queen died. It was November 26, 1504. Columbus had lost his biggest supporter.

Columbus was old and sick. His days as an explorer were over. On May 20, 1506, Christopher Columbus died. He died believing that he had found a sea route to the Indies. But he had not.

So if he didn't reach the Indies, then why is he so famous? Columbus found new lands—Caribbean islands, Jamaica, and Cuba—places that no other European had ever been to. Because of Columbus, there was now a passageway between Europe and the Americas, one that other explorers could follow.

Christopher Columbus did not find gold; instead he found a whole new world.

TIMELINE OF CHRISTOPHER COLUMBUS'S LIFE

1451 — Born in Genoa, Italy

1477 — Opens a mapmaking shop with his brother in Lisbon

1479 — Marries a noblewoman named Felipa Perestrello e Moniz

1490 — His son Diego is born

1484 — Fails to gain the patronage of King John II of Portugal

1485 — Felipa dies, and Columbus moves to Spain

1486 — Is denied support from King Ferdinand and Queen Isabella of Spain

1491 — Appeals again to Ferdinand and Isabella but is refused

1492 — King Ferdinand and Queen Isabella agree to finance Columbus's journey
On August 3, the *Niña,* the *Pinta,* and the *Santa María* set sail, heading west
Lands in the New World on October 12

1493 — Returns to Spain on March 15
Embarks on his second journey to the New World on September 25

1498 — Begins his third voyage from Spain to the New World

1500 — Arrested and sent back to Spain in chains

1502 — Fourth and final voyage of Christopher Columbus

1506 — Dies on May 20 in Spain

TIMELINE OF
THE WORLD

Marco Polo and his brother travel overland from Europe to China	1260
Competition in Florence for who will create the bronze doors for the baptistery of San Gionvanni	1401
Jan van Eyck perfects the technique of oil painting	1420
Joan of Arc is burned at the stake	1431
China ends all oversea voyages and cuts itself off from foreign visitors	1433
The Inca Empire in South America becomes the largest empire in the world	1438
Johannes Gutenberg invents the printing press	1439
The fall of Constantinople (present-day Istanbul) to the Ottoman Turks	1453
Bartholomew Diaz sails around the southern tip of Africa	1487
Ferdinand and Isabella expel all the Jews from Spain	1492
Vasco da Gama sails to India	1497
Leonardo da Vinci paints the *Mona Lisa*	1503
Construction of St. Peter's Basilica in Rome begins	1506
Michelangelo begins to paint the Sistine Chapel	1508

BIBLIOGRAPHY

Bern, Emma Carlson. **Christopher Columbus: The Voyage That Changed the World.** Sterling Publishing Co., New York: 2008.

Columbus, Christopher. **The Four Voyages of Christopher Columbus.** trans. and ed. J.M. Cohen. Penguin Books, New York: 1969.

Doak, Robin S. **Christopher Columbus: Explorer of the New World.** Compass Point Books, Minneapolis: 2005.

Fritz, Jean. **Where Do You Think You're Going, Christopher Columbus?** G.P. Putnam's Sons, New York: 1980.

McNeese, Tim. **Christopher Columbus and the Discovery of the Americas.** Chelsea House, Philadelphia: 2006.

Roop, Peter, and Connie Roop. **Christopher Columbus. In Their Own Words.** Scholastic, New York: 2000.

Sundel, Al. **Christopher Columbus and the Age of Exploration in World History.** Enslow Publishers, Berkeley Heights, NJ: 2002.